LOVED INTO LIFE

TOM WHITE

*To all who are seeking that place
where being loved by God is their home*

READER'S RESPONSE

The impact of a book is best measured by its readers

Abby is a lawyer, Linda is a mother of two. Steve is a pastor, and Chris and Laura are missionaries. We asked if they would read the manuscript before publication, and to describe how it has impacted them.

"This book helped me to know that God's life-changing love is for me personally. It has transformed my spiritual practices. I'm experiencing freedom and rest as I learn to shift away from constant striving into just wanting to be with Christ." —Abby, Lawyer

"Loved into Life beautifully explores the depths of God's love. Its pages revealed layers of truths that gently unfold, prompting a desire for deeper connection with God. The book's title perfectly describes what I am going through." —Linda, Mother and Teacher

"This is the fruit of Tom White's journey into sonship. It's a book about God revealing his nature, which is so essential, because as God reveals his love we come to receive his love.

As a hospice Chaplain, patients often ask me to convince them that God exists. I've learned I cannot do that; God must reveal himself to them. He wants to be known personally-it's why he gave us his Son so that we know and experience his love. That is what I pray for my patients. I encourage readers to ask the Lord to reveal himself personally to you, and then come to this book expecting to meet with him." —Steve, Pastor & Chaplain

"Reading this book felt like an invitation from Jesus—to be with him, to rest in his love, and to finally feel at home. It's about a journey into his love that accepts me as I am, without conditions or demands. God is calling us all to this hope; to embrace the joy and peace that in Christ we are being loved into life. —Chris and Laura, Missionaries

CONTENTS

Chapter One

SOMETHING'S MISSING

Why is it so hard sometimes to receive God's love?

That's been my prayer before the Lord: Father, how do your people open their hearts to receive the revelation of your love?

A friend once sent me a heartfelt email:

> Tom I want to ask a question about receiving God's love. Why, do you think, that it still feels like we are trying to achieve love? Or perhaps it's more an inability to receive it and just ahhhh... rest in it? Is

it too much distraction? And then how to get rid of the distraction without making it into a discipline of striving?

I can relate to this profound question. Can't you?

We hear that God loves us, but we don't experience it. We're unsure what we are doing wrong.

We try to do the right things, and believe the right things, in order to receive God's love. But the experience of his love in life isn't working out that way.

Does this sound familiar—we do things for God, we go to church, and give tithes. We sincerely believe that Jesus died for our sins. We experience God's blessed nearness during worship.

Most sermons speak about God's grace and truth, and at the end the pastor exhorts us to go forth and do. We head home resolved to do better.

But in our daily lives we're often stressed. We strive and multi-task at most things. Inside we are anxious and a bit lonely. But then we're frustrated for feeling this way; after all we're not supposed to feel like this!

If a brother or sister comes along and tells us that God loves us, we may nod our head. But what they're saying can seem like a fantasy. If it's really true, then why do I feel left out, because it's not what I experience?

If this sounds like what you've been through at times, may I say that I understand. I've lived through this, and I've been there myself.

As a pastor of a nondenominational Protestant church, I built a serious "working relationship" with God. I did things for God. I believed the right things about God. I worked so that everyone in church—especially my family and I—would experience the right things from God.

Our community did receive blessings, and in those moments of 'reward' we experienced his grace. But the moments didn't last. Soon we returned back to old familiar strivings.

It was only when I couldn't work any longer, and I stopped "working" for God, that I slowly began to realize I had been thinking completely wrong.

I had been building a "transactional relationship" with God that was far more distant and impersonal than it was personal.

Let me explain.

Transactional Relationships

What do we mean by "transactional relationships"? Perhaps an example from the business world might help.

Sales are booming at Sewell Automotive, America's second largest Cadillac dealership. Years ago Carl Sewell created a business model whose aim is not to sell you a car, like every other dealership. His goal is for you to buy every car you'll ever own from him.

"Building relationships, not selling cars and trucks, is our first priority." This is Carl's mission statement. It's a model of customer service so successful, that he wrote the book *Customers for Life: How to Turn That One-Time Buyer Into a Lifetime Customer*.

Carl offers a personal relationship which is built on a transaction: If you buy cars from me, I will take good care of you for life.

This sounds eerily like my personal relationship with God.

I thought God was saying "If you do the right things, I will take care of you for life."

It's so natural to assume that in order to please God, we ought to be doing the right things. We ought to be believing the right things. And we ought to be experiencing the right things. Do the right things, believe the right things, experience the right things—and God will take care of you for life.

It has the feel of a transaction.

Now transactional relationships are normal and useful. They're everywhere in life. Society runs on transactional relationships. Some are formal and impersonal; others are personal and friendly. But whether impersonal or personal, the relationship works on the transaction "If you give me what I ask, I will give you what you ask in return."

So is it possible that we've assumed that a personal relationship with God is also transactional? Like many of our social and interpersonal relationships?

Could the assumed transactional relationship with God be clouding our understanding of his nature?

Hindering us from receiving the love which he has for us?!

Let's examine three ways we often assume God's love is transactional.

God loves me on the basis of what I do

We tend to think that relationship with God is based on what we Christians do—mostly in church on Sunday. We sing praise and worship songs, we pray and intercede for the world. We offer our money, our time and talents.

We sit listening as the pastor "does his thing", exhorting us "to do our thing". Jesus teaches us what to do and leaves us an example of how to do it. No doubt we need God's grace to help us do it.

We can view personal relationship with God as essentially a series of transactions, from which we either gain or lose by what we do.

It's often similar to the way we interact with parents, teachers, employers, and perhaps even our spouse!

Has our *doing* for God become the unspoken reason whether he loves us or not? Has performance become the unspoken arbitrator of whether he loves us?

Isn't there some deeper, more fundamental assurance that's missing in all this?

If our relationship with God is built on doing things for him, might that "thinking" be part of what hinders us from knowing and experiencing his love?

God loves me on the basis of how I believe

We all understand how precious the gift of faith is. We cherish it. Believing in Christ's saving work is knowing we are accepted by God.

The expressions "saved by the gospel", "saved by faith alone", and "the saving power of the cross" all declare glorious truths about God's work of salvation.

But, very subtly, is it possible to assume that our faith in Christ's work is the virtue which causes Christ's gifts to be gifted to us? That our faith is what makes us worthy of salvation?

Is it my faith in the work of Christ that causes Christianity to "work"? If it is my faith that causes salvation, then I will undertake a devoted exercise of will to believe.

I will exercise my will to believe, and how well I believe determines how strong my faith in God is. And that strength of my faith will cause God to do mighty things.

For many years I lived under this assumption. After all isn't what I believe and how I believe—that is, my belief system—the key to unlocking the kingdom of God?!

Early in our walk with the Lord, my wife and I were drawn into the personal charisma of a Texas pastor, who proclaimed through many passages of Scripture that faith is the key to unlocking the power of the kingdom of God. Any problems we experienced in life, whether sickness or lack of finances, was due to our lack of faith.

He said "If you drove up to church tonight in a Volkswagen, it's because you don't have faith for a Cadillac."

I remember that night driving out of the parking lot, thinking that my car said a lot about my lack of faith.

When we assume that being loved by God depends on how strong our faith is in Christ's works, what happens when we doubt? Or when our prayers are not answered, or when we don't know what to believe? Or when we simply don't believe?

If love from God depends on how well I believe, isn't there something deeply disturbing about that?

Shouldn't there be a deeper assurance that's not secured by my faith alone? That does not depend upon my force of will to believe?

Has a transactional relationship with God clouded our understanding of faith?

Could we have lost sight of the truth that our faith in him is gifted to us, and perfected in us, by its Author and Perfecter? (Hebrews 12:21)

God loves me on the basis
of what I experience

We tend to think that personal relationship with God is conditional on what we experience. Christianity is about how we experience life in a Christian way.

In particular, we can assume that our relationship with God is grounded on what we emotionally experience.

We relate to him on the basis of how we feel. After all, Scripture says "Delight yourself in the Lord, and he will give you the desires of your heart." (Psalm 37:4)

We conclude that the love of God is a continuous set of good experiences from God. His love empowers our self-esteem, self-worth, self-identity. The God-given feeling of human potential and possibility is validated when we feel his love.

It's very easy to slip into this kind of thinking. It's actually more non-relational than we realize. Because if God's love is about how it makes me feel, isn't the relationship with God basically about wanting to feel good about myself?!

What happens when we're feeling a bit depressed or lonely?

Does God love us less because we feel this way?

Is he disappointed with us?

Or where is God when "I am just not feeling him"?

Please don't misunderstand what I am saying. God made us to experience the truth through a wealth of emotions in the renewing of our mind. The fruits of the Spirit burst with emotions and truth. God says "Come take delight in me, for at my right hand are pleasures forevermore." (Psalm 16:11)

When we assume that our emotional experiences are the judge of whether God loves us or not; when we see God's love as conditional, based on what we experience; that's a sign we may be relating with him through transactions.

Here's an all too common scenario that comes from this thinking. Say you're someone who normally doesn't have deep emotional experiences while worshiping in church.

You're not "feeling it" like others around you.

Do you sometimes feel left behind because you're not experiencing God like they are—or maybe even as they imply you ought?!

Has an assumption crept in, that you're not as close to God as you should be, simply because your experience is different?

Something is missing

There *is* something missing when transactional assumptions about a 'personal relationship' with God holds sway. Even if we got every doing and believing and experiencing right, there would still be something missing.

For example, what happens when you're sick, or when you have evil thoughts, or do something wrong (yet again), or you're not thinking about God at all?

If it's all up to you, and you are not doing the right thing, where are you with God? For that matter, where is God?!

It's no wonder many sincere Christians are striving, anxious, and lonely in their walk with the Lord. And this includes pastors, ministry leaders and missionaries!

If this sounds all too familiar, can I say that there is actually very good news in all of this! What if it is **our assumptions** about how God relates to us, that is at the heart of the problem?

Could we be thinking partially right in some ways about God, but just downright wrong in others?

Have we built an impersonal, transactional concept of God, where he relates to us based on whether we've done, believed, or experienced the right things?

Because if we have, then it's no wonder there's trouble receiving God's love. Our "transactions" simply do not determine whether God loves us or not.

Indeed we might experience true religious affections in a transactional relationship; but God's love is something far deeper than the limited satisfaction of thinking that we've secured God's approval by doing or feeling right things.

When God revealed to me how the striving, fear, and loneliness I lived with came from wrong transactional assumptions about his nature—the reality came in waves of seismic relief! The struggle to know God's love wasn't coming from God or the Holy Spirit. The problem was with me!

I had assumed that almost everything God required for true relationship was being thrown back upon me to do and believe and experience. I assumed this is how you relate to God. Yes there's grace, but you have to do it more or less on your own.

Sounds rather transactional, doesn't it? Human assumptions creep into our relationship with the Lord. And yes, that's painful to face head-on and admit.

But the very good news in all this, is that a transactional relationship is not what God requires. It is not God's nature, it is not God's gospel, and it is not the foundation of God's love.

Let me restate this hope at the risk of repetition: our concepts and assumptions about "personal relationship" can be flawed—hiding the true nature of the Lord, whose love is sovereign, secure, and beautiful beyond description.

So the problem lies with us, not with God. And that is such very good news!

Instead, Jesus invites us to come and be with him, in order to know him relationally:

> Come to me, all you who are weary and burdened, and I will give you rest. Take my yoke upon you and learn from me, for I am gentle and humble in heart, and you will find rest for your souls. For my yoke is easy and my burden is light.
>
> Matthew 11:28-30

Just learning to be with Jesus. Learning from *him*. His words are pure, peaceable, and gentle. The Good Shepherd is open to reason. He is full of mercy and good fruits. He's impartial and sincere. (James 3:17)

We enter a rest—his rest—that restores our souls. (Psalm 23:3)

Isn't Jesus gently leading us out of our old transactional assumptions? Leading us into something more real and true. Something which grounds the substance of our faith and hope.

Something which leads us to form a new set of assumptions:

That I could be loved—without having to be good enough?

That I could be loved—without having to merit it on my own?

That I could be loved—without having to do anything for it?

Neither do I condemn you

Consider the woman caught in adultery, recorded in John 8:2-11. As Jesus was teaching the people in the temple in Jerusalem, the scribes and Pharisees brought a woman caught in adultery before Jesus, and placed her in the midst of them.

> They said to him, "Teacher, this woman has been caught in the act of adultery. Now in the Law, Moses commanded us to stone such women. So what do you say?" They said this to test him, that they might

have some charge to bring against him. Jesus bent down and wrote with his finger on the ground. And as they continued to ask him, he stood up and said to them, "Let him who is without sin among you be the first to throw a stone at her." And once more he bent down and wrote on the ground. But when they heard it, they went away one by one, beginning with the older ones, and Jesus was left alone with the woman standing before him. Jesus stood up and said to her, "Woman, where are they? Has no one condemned you?" She said, "No one, Lord." And Jesus said, "Neither do I condemn you; go, and from now on sin no more."

John 8:2-11

At the temple in Jerusalem stood a man who possessed greater authority than Moses. The Son of Man. The Son of God. The only man among them all without sin, who did not throw the first stone at her.

Jesus broke the judgment of death over her, silencing her accusers. He spoke, and mercy triumphed over judgment.

Her sentence of death was exchanged for a sentence of life.

> Neither do I condemn you; go, and from now on sin no more.

For the woman her deliverance was intensely personal. She had met the Author of Life, who exchanged mercy and life for a transaction of judgment and death. She would never be the same!

As this woman experienced the Savior's love, so do we now with our exalted Lord Jesus Christ. He guides us into growing revelations of personal hope:

*That you **are** loved—without having to be good enough!*

*That you **are** loved—without having to merit it on your own!*

*That you **are** loved—without having to do anything but receive!*

Transactional relationships are normal and necessary in life. Society, governments, businesses all function because of them.

It's when we consider what is missing in transactional relationships—that deeper, more foundational, more necessary, more constant, relational love.

Something which the heart of every human longs for and struggles to find.

Author PB North touched upon this sense of "being loved" in one of his novels. A middle-aged widower discovers a love that he thought was forever lost to him, entering his life like the rays of the morning sun:

> It's that moment when things stop being difficult. When you stop being nervous, or insecure. When you feel safe with someone, as if it's easier to be with them than away from them. Have you ever felt that? It's like coming home.
>
> PB North

We're going to journey next into the personal relationship that our Lord calls us to.

My sincere prayer is that it will be like coming home for you as well.

Chapter Two

WHO DO YOU SAY I AM?

Asking God who he really is, is not presumptuous. It is humble and honest. It's wanting to know who he is personally.

"Who are you...to me?" is more about relationship than asking questions like what are you, or how are you, or why are you. These come in their time.

But the key question for knowing God is "*Who*".

In the end it's not what I know about God that matters. It's *Who* knows me, and makes himself known to me that matters the most.

One afternoon I chanced to run into my friend Paul, from church. We met in a parking lot close to a coffee shop, and as we both had time, we went in for a coffee to catch up.

Paul is one of those people you just like being around. He's laid back, interesting. A pleasure to talk with. He loves the Lord and easily shares the good things in life.

As we were chatting, he chanced to look past me to the entrance, and a change suddenly came over him. He stiffened, and the smile left his face. I turned and saw his 20 year old son standing in line.

The next few minutes were a bit awkward. Paul was cordial but frosty, and distracted. I tried to keep things light. His son eventually got his coffee, came over and said hello briefly, and left.

Paul relaxed.

After a pause I asked "Paul, what was that all about?!" He looked at me wearily. "It's a long story. Probably not something we should talk about here." I asked if we could meet somewhere private and he jumped at the opportunity.

We met about a week later and Paul told his story.

He described the ways his son frustrated and disappointed him. He was rebellious. He didn't accept his authority. He didn't respect his mother, he didn't take advice. It seemed that his son could never do enough to please Paul.

As he wound up recounting the troubles caused by his son, I asked him how it was growing up with his own father. Paul's anger shifted seamlessly from the present to his past.

Paul's dad was most often away from home. He travelled on the road as a salesman six days a week. Paul wouldn't see him for days. When he did come home, they spent little time together.

Paul mostly remembers his dad getting angry at him for not helping his mother around the house. For not taking his school work seriously. In time Paul disliked being around him.

I asked if there might be a connection between the alienation with his father, and the relationship he had with his son.

The thought jolted Paul. Was there a connection between Paul's father, and the way Paul was treating his son? Might there be more to his anger than just his son's behavior that was disappointing him?

It was compelling to Paul and he thanked me. He felt better for having talked it out.

I told him how much I appreciated him, and what he had shared with me. Then I said, "Paul, have you ever told our heavenly Father what you just told me?"

He looked at me with surprise. "No." Then he paused; "I never thought of that."

I said "It's true God knows everything about us. He knows us better than we know ourselves. But there's something about telling him personally. It's important to him that we tell him. He wants us to share our history. To connect with him. Why not share with him just like you did with me."

Paul paused for a few moments. He said he'd think about it.

Two weeks later I met Paul again. His friendly smile was back, and it seemed richer and deeper. There was light in his eyes. He said that he told God his story.

That had started a conversation, and it opened up more and more things. He said "I didn't realize how deeply God knows me. I didn't realize how near he is. I didn't know how much he cares.

And my son and I are talking for the first time."

Jesus asks a question

> When Jesus came to the region of Cae-
> sarea Philippi, he asked his disciples,
> "Who do people say the Son of Man is?"
> They replied, "Some say John the Baptist;
> others say Elijah; and still others, Jeremiah
> or one of the prophets."
>
> Matthew 16:13-18

Jesus and his disciples had just left Capernaeum and
travelled through the region of Galilee. They were
headed to the northern village of Caesarea Philippi.

Wherever Jesus went the region buzzed with aston-
ishment. Powerful acts of God manifested in the midst
of humble villages. People were amazed by miracles,
and astonished by his teaching because his words carried authority.

Jesus knew that people everywhere were engaged in
spirited debate about him. Who is he, and where did
the power to do and say such things come from? He

turned to his disciples and asked them "Who do people say the Son of Man is?"

His disciples related that opinions were widespread. Some claimed he was John the Baptist, others said Elijah, and still others Jeremiah or one of the prophets. Actually no one knew for sure. Everyone was guessing.

But they did know this for a fact—many sick people were now healed and rejoicing and telling everybody about their good fortune! Because of these miracles, multitudes from the surrounding villages were bringing their sick and suffering to Jesus, desperate to gain deliverance for themselves.

Knowing fully the effect he had upon the villagers, Jesus turned and asked his disciples:

> But what about you? Who do you say I am?
> Matthew 16:15

He waited for their response.

I believe that moment must have been quite personal for the disciples. They, like the townspeople, were trying to understand who Jesus was. They'd seen and witnessed him do so many miracles and heard his astonishing teaching. But now Jesus was asking them to disclose to him who he is—to them, and for them.

But what about you...who do *you* say I am?

We're not told how long it took the disciples to respond. But we know that Simon Peter eventually did.

I sometimes wonder whether Peter thought back to one of his first encounters with Jesus. He had watched him teach a large crowd gathered on the shoreline, while Jesus stood in Peter's boat. When he had finished teaching, he turned to Simon and asked him to put out into deeper water, and let down his nets for a catch. "Master, we've worked hard all night and haven't caught anything...but at your word I will let down the nets."

Peter let down his nets into deeper water. And suddenly, everything that this fisherman had struggled for all night was gifted to him, in an explosion of abundance!

The miracle stunned the fishermen.

Peter turned and stared at Jesus. Jesus gazed upon Peter. It seems in that moment the Son of God revealed to Peter who he was. Jesus, sitting in his boat. Looking at him.

In the face of this man Jesus, Peter knew he was looking at the face of God.

He fell at Jesus' knees, "Depart from me, for I am a sinful man, O Lord." Jesus said "Don't be afraid; from now on you will be catching men." Simon Peter left his boats and everything and followed him. (Luke 5:1-11)

Once again Jesus looked at his disciples, and awaited their response.

> Simon Peter answered, "You are the Messiah, the Son of the living God." Jesus replied, "Blessed are you, Simon son of Jonah, for this was not revealed to you by flesh and blood, but by my Father in heaven."
>
> Matthew 16:15

The Father had revealed Jesus, his Beloved Son to Peter! As if the Father had said "This is my Son. The one whom I love. With him I am well pleased."

And the Son of God looked at Peter, and said:

> And I tell you that you are Peter, and on
> this rock I will build my church, and the
> gates of Hades will not overcome it.
>   Matthew 16:18

Jesus *knew* Peter. Had known him before Peter saw who he was. "Son of Jonah, I know you. I tell you that you are Peter."

No matter how many mistakes he would make, Peter was assured of divine connection—he was known by the Son of God. Not distantly, but by his name.

As the Father revealed Jesus as the Christ to Peter, so it is for everyone to whom the Father reveals his Beloved Son.

No matter how many mistakes we make, no matter how many doubts we have or unbelief we keep from him, God assures us of divine love and connection. He knows us by name, and we know him by name.

Upon this rock Christ will build his church, and the gates of Hades will not overcome it.

Who do you say I am?

In our life as Christians we come into the knowledge of Christ in a variety of ways. By the working of the Word and the Spirit. Sensing his presence in worship, in preaching, in prayer and intercession. In fellowship with brothers and sisters. Throughout the circumstances of our lives, in our daily routines and personal history.

Each of us carry an impression or conception of God, which we mostly keep to ourselves. It's the knowledge of God that we keep as we go about everyday life, with its ups and downs.

It's our understanding of who God is, when we're not thinking about him.

It's these personal understandings about God, which the Lord summons us to share with him. Through the Holy Spirit God asks us "In this situation you're facing right now, who do you say I am?"

Oftentimes, when we stop to consider that question, it's quite easy to misinterpret it. We assume that he's asking "*What can I do for you?*"

"Hmmm, what can you do for me?! Good question. I could use the raise I've been promised. And you know I need a Cadillac. I need my children to be better behaved, especially at church." I know that God will provide for all my needs. I'll keep on praying, trusting that he'll come through.

It's so easy to slip into a transactional relationship with God without realizing it! By altering God's question from "Who do you say I am " to "What can I do for you" the relationship becomes transactional.

But look at the question he's asking:

Who do *you* say that I am...?

Do I know what's on your heart ....?

Am I good...to you?

Do I know what you're going through...?

Am I with you...?

Do I care....?

Do you want to hear what I say....?

Doesn't Christ's question compel us to enter more honestly into personal relationship?

Our responses will expose the concepts we carry about God—right, wrong, good, bad, spot on or off base. He wants us to confide what we carry.

That's the gentle persuasion of "Who do you say I am."

A few years ago, I needed to ask God a question which had been troubling me for some time. The problem was that I was too afraid to go and ask.

I'd suppress the question, and it would go away for a time. Then it would return, and I'd suppress it again.

But during a particularly challenging season my need to hear from God came with such urgency that I had no choice but to go and ask.

So with a bit of trembling I began "Father God, you are so busy. You're doing many good things all over the world. You're saving people and blessing many. But I just wanted to ask... do you have any time for me?"

A moment of silence. Then I 'heard' (thought?, experienced?) his reply "Son, I've been waiting for you to ask me that question for a long time."

I was stunned. It was not what I expected! He continued,

"You see son, I am Spirit (John 4:24). Because I am Spirit I can be everywhere at once (Psalm 139:8-10). I am good. I am a perfect Father, to all of my children, all of the time. So you see my son, I have all the time in the world for you."

A huge burden fell off of me, and a stream of affection and peace flowed in like living water. I felt I was drinking living water and getting showered by it at the same time!

My first human response? I slapped my hand on the table and said "Darn! Why hadn't I asked him that question years ago?!"

God had been waiting for me to ask him, and tell him what I carried. He knew I kept it from him. And he wanted to lift the burden. But I had to go to him and ask.

It's relational. I had to bring my doubts and fears to him. What others say is nice but it doesn't really cut it. He's the only one who could answer that question, and I needed to hear his response.

Moments later, as I was processing what I had heard, the Lord gently spoke "Come spend time with me. I'll teach you how to stay near." And he took me into Scripture,

> I will instruct you and teach you in the way you should go; I will counsel you with my eye upon you. Be not like a horse or a mule, without understanding, which must be curbed with bit and bridle, or it will not stay near you.
>
> Psalm 32:8-9

I believe that Jesus is teaching us that through confiding our honest thoughts and intentions, he comes and reveals his truth and love.

The exchange creates an ever deepening relationship, delivering us from ourselves alone, into communion in relationship with the living God.

Consider how friendships develop. People share what they think and feel. They reveal their thoughts—past and present, their ups and downs. Their hopes and dreams.

As they listen to one another, the relationship grows through a flow of mutual understanding, and hopefully trust and respect. The friendship deepens.

Consider how people fall in love. Isn't it because they "discover" the attractiveness of the other? They reveal and share who they truly are. As they come to know the answer to "Who is this woman?" and "Who is this man?", the discovery of their value—and the value they give—is what makes love "happen".

If sharing who we are, and what we're thinking deepens human relationships, wouldn't sharing who we are, and what we're thinking reveal to us a profound reality?

That Christ is *actively listening* to us?!

Years ago there were times I'd come home from work to find that my wife had a particularly rough day with our young children. We'd go for a walk down the street, and she'd unload her problems. In quite some detail. As I listened I'd mentally make a list of how to fix those problems.

When the majority of her venting subsided, I'd tell her how I would deal with the children once we were back home, and that would really upset her! She'd say to me "You're not listening!"

"Yes I am!" I'd reply. And I would assure her that I had been listening by explaining again what I'd do when we got home. She would get so frustrated: "You're not listening *to me*!"

I felt misunderstood and unappreciated. At first. It took a while, but I began to realize she was right in what she said.

I really wasn't listening to *her*. I was listening to all her problems, and all the things I must do.

She was trying to tell me that she didn't want fixing, she wanted my companionship. She wanted someone who understood how tired and frustrated she was. Someone who wouldn't judge her for feeling that way. She wanted someone she could share life with.

Eventually I learned to put away my to-do agenda, learning instead how to just be with her. To be with her and actively listen without being distracted by having to fix it. That's what she was after! Those evening walks became something we both looked forward to.

Being with someone just to listen to them. *Seeing* them through what they are sharing. Giving them the space to be who they are, so they know they are heard and understood.

This kind of "active listening" doesn't just express love, it is love. You value them by listening; you listen because you value them.

God actively listens to you and me, and we can actively listen to him. And we don't have to wait until an evening walk to do that. We can be actively listening to each other throughout the day!

Revelation through relationship

Jesus summons us to be honest with him in personal relationship, so that we can receive revelations which we didn't know or realize.

Look what the Apostle Paul prayed in Ephesians:

> ...that the God of our Lord Jesus Christ, the Father of glory, may give you the Spirit of wisdom and of revelation in the knowledge of him, having the eyes of your hearts enlightened, that you may know what is the hope to which he has called you.
>
> Ephesians 1:16-18

The Greek word for **knowledge** which Paul uses here is *epiginosis*, which means "personal knowledge gained by experience and participation". Paul prays we experience and participate by knowing God *firsthand*.

Secondhand knowledge of something can't take the place of experiencing it—firsthand. You can know about jumping out of airplanes by taking classes. But you'll never **know** skydiving until you throw yourself out of the plane.

In the same way, we cannot live only from second-hand knowledge of God. While Scripture contains the truth about Christ, it is relationally knowing Christ that causes us to live.

We need to know *firsthand* that God truly forgives us and reconciles us to himself. We need to know *firsthand* that he truly loves us by experiencing his mercy and love.

People ask to experience God's love so often, because they need to know that he loves them—*firsthand!* The living God has so fashioned our hearts that we long to know our Father's love. We will be restless until we *know* that!

> O God, you are my God; earnestly I seek you, my soul thirsts for you; my flesh faints for you, as in a dry and weary land where there is no water.
>
> Psalm 63:1

Seeking us, seeking him

It's a wonder that God would enable us to know him *by seeking us first*!

> Behold, I stand at the door and knock. If anyone hears my voice and opens the door, I will come in to him and eat with him, and he with me.
>
> Revelation 3:20

Christ takes the initiative to seek you out. Knocking and calling to you by name. Asking you to invite him in to share a meal together.

And God summons us to seek him out.

> You have said, "Seek my face." My heart says to you, "Your face, Lord, do I seek."
>
> Psalm 27:8

And I tell you, ask, and it will be given to you; seek, and you will find; knock, and it will be opened to you. For everyone who asks receives, and the one who seeks, finds, and to the one who knocks it will be opened.

Luke 11:9-10

Ask, Seek, Knock. And Receive, Discover, Enter in.

God wants you to know him *firsthand*.

Be kind. Everyone you meet is carrying a heavy burden...This man beside us also has a hard fight with an unfavoring world, with strong temptations, with doubts and fears, with wounds of the past which have skinned over, but which smart when they are touched...And when this occurs to us we are moved to deal kindly with him, to bid him understand that we are also fighting a battle.

Ian Maclaren

Everyone, whether we realize it or not, is searching for something. Everyone carries a burden which is often unseen by people around them. I saw a poster which captured this with wry humor:

> Every 10 seconds someone discovers that we're all in this together.

May our Lord Jesus bless you by finding what you're looking for: may you hear him calling your name.

Knowing that he wants you to know him. That he's pleased to know you.

May you increasingly find those quiet moments with him, when life stops being difficult. When you stop being nervous, or insecure. When you feel safe because of his nearness. As if it's easier to be with him than away from him.

May it be to you like you've come home.

Chapter Three

ARE YOU THIRSTY?

Throughout Scripture God calls us to do something. He calls us to come to him and drink. He promises to give us a special kind of water. When we drink of this water, a deep-seated need is satisfied.

The water's effect is good and refreshing. It causes us to just enjoy, give thanks, and abide in it. And we want to drink more. So we come to God and drink—and our lives are made better for it. The water he gives just somehow makes life better.

What is this water, which satisfies us? Which causes us to thirst for more What is this deep-seated need in us, which is satisfied somehow by the water which God provides?

> On the last day of the feast, the great day,
> Jesus stood up and cried out, "If anyone
> thirsts, let him come to me and drink.
> Whoever believes in me, as the Scripture
> has said, 'Out of his innermost being will
> flow rivers of living water.'"
>
> John 7:37-38

Jesus cried out these authoritative words on the very last day of the Feast of Tabernacles. The feast had already been underway for seven days. And during the morning of each festival day, the High Priest performed the same ceremony, joined by the thousands of pilgrims who had gathered in Jerusalem.

In light of this repeated ceremony, the astonished crowd would have immediately grasped the meaning of Jesus' shocking claim when he stood up on the last day and cried out. Because the ceremony each morning of the feast was thanking God for satisfying Israel's thirst!

Let's take a brief look at this ceremony.

The water pouring ceremony

Each morning the High Priest and the gathered pilgrims performed the "water pouring ceremony". The Priest ceremoniously carried a golden vessel from the temple to the Siloam stream, which was about 300 meters away. The Siloam stream was known as "the sweet and abundant fountain", and its fresh water was believed to have healing and cleansing power.

Thousands of pilgrims accompanied the High Priest as he made his way to the Siloam stream. It was a procession of joy, as trumpets blared, people shouted, sang, and clapped hands.

The people grew silent as the priest knelt at the stream and filled the vessel. He then stood, and lifting the vessel, he returned to the temple. The crowd followed him singing words from Isaiah:

> Surely God is my salvation; I will trust and
> not be afraid.
> The Lord, the Lord himself, is my strength
> and my defense;

> he has become my salvation.
> With joy you will draw water from the
> wells of salvation.
>
> Isaiah 12:2-3

The High Priest then entered the temple through the "Water Gate", named after this ceremony. As he approached the altar, the people cried out to the priest, "Raise your hand!" The priest raised his hand high and poured out water upon the altar.

The "water pouring ceremony" enacted God's promises to Israel as recorded in Isaiah 12. Drawing water from the Siloam stream represented drawing water from the wells of salvation. The High Priest pouring water on the altar symbolized God giving life and salvation to his people.

Thousands of pilgrims at the Feast rejoiced in drawing from the wells of salvation.

It was in the charged atmosphere of this celebration that Jesus stood and cried out in a loud voice "If anyone thirsts, let him come to me and drink."

The High Priest and pilgrims would have been shocked. At this sacred gathering of all places, Jesus declared that the "water pouring ceremony" was about him! They were celebrating the water Jesus gives to those who thirst, and come to him for drink. Jesus is the Siloam stream. He is the source of living water. He is Israel's well of salvation.

He then declared:

> Whoever believes in me, as the Scripture has said, "Out of his innermost being will flow rivers of living water."
>
> John 7:38

A divine life-connection will occur between Jesus and those who come to him to drink. *From Christ's innermost being, rivers of living water will flow into them*!

His living water will quench a deep thirst that they carry. Refreshing their inner being. Causing them to worship with joy!

This is the blessing God foretold through the prophet Isaiah:

> For I give water in the wilderness, rivers in the desert, to give drink to my chosen people, the people whom I formed for myself that they might declare my praise.
>
> Isaiah 43:19-20

The apostle John, then explained to his reader's what is this living water that Christ referred to:

> By this he meant the Spirit, whom those who believed in him were later to receive. Up to that time the Spirit had not been given, since Jesus had not yet been glorified.
>
> John 7:39

John makes the connection between the living water Jesus spoke of, and the Holy Spirit. The water and the Spirit are often the same in Scripture, as we read of its outpouring in Isaiah:

> For I will pour **water** on him who is thirsty, And floods on the dry ground; I will pour My **Spirit** on your descendants, And My blessing on your offspring;
>
> Isaiah 44:3

So the outpouring of living water and the outpouring of the Spirit of God are synonymous.

Let's go a bit deeper into this, and consider some important questions. What happens within us when we come to Christ and drink of this living water?

What is the effect of this living water upon us, as Christ pours his Spirit—from his innermost being—into us?

Within our humanity, what is it in us which is so satisfied by this living water?

What is the effect that causes us to want to drink more and more of it?!

These are significant questions, because they speak to the mystery of *how* God the Spirit ministers personal relationship with Christ to us.

In the upper room, on the night before he was cruci-
fied, Christ promised his disciples that he would ask
the Father to send another Helper, the Spirit of truth.
And in promising this, he then made this startling
statement:

> I will not leave you as orphans; I will come
> to you.
>
> John 14:16 -18

I will not leave you as orphans—*I will personally
come to you.* I am leaving, and it's to your advantage
that I go away. But then I will come to you. You have
to wait just a bit.

And so the disciples waited. Then at Pentecost—*Jesus
returned!*

The disciples instantly knew something profound and
transformative had happened to them. One moment
they were ordinary men, awaiting a promise. The next
moment, the life of the living Christ flowed into them,
coursing into them like rivers of living water.

Jesus had returned! They would never be alone or on their own again.

In this fulfilled promise, Peter then told the astonished crowd observing all of this:

> Being therefore exalted at the right hand of God, and having received from the Father the promise of the Holy Spirit, he (Jesus) has poured out this that you yourselves are seeing and hearing.
>
> Acts 2:33

Through the outpouring of living water—the promised Holy Spirit—Jesus returned to them. He came and joined them to himself.

A profound identity shift began to occur in them—they were no longer orphans. Christ joined them to his life. They were sons of God in him.

❖❖ ⋯ ⋅◆⋅ ⋯ ❖❖

So, what is this living water that Jesus pours out on us?

I wonder if it isn't the very life of the risen Lord Jesus. His life given to us by the Spirit, who joins us to Christ in a communion of fellowship in his body.

His life poured into us through the Holy Spirit. His life flowing into us, joining us in communion with himself in his body.

Bidding us to come believe in him, to find life in him—not apart from him in self alone. Believing in him more and more. Receiving him more and more. Learning to drink more and more with joy from the well of salvation.

As Jesus told the Samaritan woman at the well:

> ...but those who drink of the water that I will give them will never be thirsty. The water that I will give will become in them a spring of water gushing up to eternal life.
>
> John 4:14

This living relationship which Christ gives is so richly expressed in John Chapter 15:

> I am the vine; you are the branches. Whoever abides in me and I in him, he it is that bears much fruit, for apart from me you can do nothing.
>
> John 15:5

Christ joins us to himself by the Spirit. We branches are attached to his life-giving vine.

Because we are joined to the life of the vine, we drink from the vine. And as we drink, Christ pours his life into us. It's a reciprocal relational dynamic of receiving and giving between the branch and the vine. We drink life from the vine. As we drink, the flow of Christ's life nourishes our humanity, satisfying us with his life.

Perhaps an analogy might help. Consider how a newborn baby is nourished. The baby is introduced to the mother's bosom, and the newborn begins to drink.

Nourishment flows from mother to baby. The newborn drinks in life, and the mother gives out life. Drinking causes the baby to receive life— then in satisfaction the baby enters a rest and grows from the life it receives.

As we drink life from the vine, his life is joined relationally with ours by the Holy Spirit. We are deeply satisfied by receiving the substance of a life far better than ours alone.

We receive the blessing of knowing Christ as Person. Of being known by him. Hearing him call you by name. Hearing his voice explaining truth by his words. Knowing he abides in you and with you, and calls you his friend.

Jesus said:

> Because I live, you also will live. On that day you will know that I am in My Father, and you are in Me, and I am in you.
>
> John 14:19-20

Isn't that what we all thirst for—life from him, and life with him?!

Experiencing a newness of eternal life that he shares with us?

A life that fills us not just for a Sunday morning, but for Monday mornings, and every day, as he teaches us to live through him in this world.

With such a call to live with and through the ascended Lord Jesus Christ—what else can we do but lift up the cup of our salvation—and receive!

Chapter Four

STUCK AT THE CROSSROADS

The day was darkening as a young man in a field strained against the muddy clods with a shovel. The dirt sucked at his boots as the drizzle settled over the countryside that November evening.

Not far away lay the family homestead. A man stepped out onto the porch and yelled out to the young man "It's time to come home."

"I'll be there in a minute" cried the young man as he pulled at a large stone stuck in the muck of the back acreage.

Thirty minutes later the man opened the door and stepped out again onto the porch. "Dinner's almost ready."

"Give me a minute" yelled the young man as he redoubled his efforts to dislodge a large rock.

Time passed and a cold mist settled onto the night. The porch door opened a third time, and the man's frame silhouetted in the light of the door. "Dinner is on the table" he called out into the darkness.

The young man straightened his aching back and stared at the distant light. Leaning on his shovel he whispered "I can't." Then he yelled out "I can't! I can't come home! I DON'T KNOW HOW!"

The man on the porch stared out into the darkness. Then slowly he turned around, went back into the house, and closed the door.

The young man had never been so alone. Staring at the ground, exhausted and sore, he groaned "What am I going to do? Where do I go? I can't go home. Where do I spend the night?" Time passed as he leaned on his shovel, stuck in the field. He had no answers.

A noise in the darkness startled him; it was the sound of boots sucked by the mud. Someone was approaching from the direction of the house. "Don't be afraid. I'm coming to... woah, look at all the rocks you cleared! But your hands, they're blistered."

"Yeah" said the young man, "I've been clearing rocks since dawn, but every time I clear one I find two more."

"Here," said the man, "Give me your shovel."

Taking it in his left hand he gently offered his right arm. "You must be tired. Come lean against me. Our saplings will bloom in this field come spring. We can plant them together!"

"That would be amazing" said the young man, relieved at the prospect of working with him.

And though they were both wet from the cold mist, they stood chatting about the new season, talking farming strategies, trading stories, enjoying a laugh every now and then. The young man was profoundly grateful for the man's presence. He breathed warmth and life into him in the darkness of the field.

Soon with arms intertwined they made their way as one across the fields. With each step, the young man felt lighter and stronger, as the mud on the boots of both men fell away.

As they approached the homestead, the man from the house stepped out again onto the porch. The young man cried out with joy as he raced up the porch steps,

"I'm home! Dad I'm home. Jesus brought me home!" as he ran into his father's arms.

"I've been waiting for you son. Come, we're very glad you're home."

The young man entered his homestead and looked into the dining room. Sitting at the table, his brothers and sisters turned and cried out with joy. They hadn't begun eating! "We couldn't start without you. It wouldn't be the same. Come let's celebrate!"

Taking his place at the table, the young man looked across the banquet at the uniqueness of each brother and sister. They blessed each other, and gave thanks to the One who made this all possible.

As they prayed the young man glanced back into the hallway. The Father and the Son were talking; then the Father smiled and embraced the Son, and the Son embraced the Father.

And the house lit up in the radiance of the glory that flowed between them.

Seeing this, the young man understood. His work hadn't brought him home. Jesus had come into the night and met him in the darkness where he was stuck. He took the shovel from his blistered hands, and gave him the strength of his arm to lean on. His weakness fell away in the ease of Christ's divine humanity, as he experienced the love of Christ flowing into him.

It was that same love he saw flowing between Father and Son. That same love had found him in the field, had strengthened him, and brought him home.

As Jesus took his place at the table, the young man caught his eye and quietly said "You are my Messiah, my Savior and Lord. Thank you."

Jesus smiled at him in return.

I have loved you

> The Lord came to us from far away, saying,
> "I have loved you with a love that lasts
> forever. So I have helped you come to me
> with loving-kindness."
>
> Jeremiah 31:3

What makes God's love so riveting is the internal effect it has on the one he cares about. Each time we are touched by a connection with Christ's life, we are changed by the love we receive. He lifts us out of experiencing life alone, into experiencing a life lived through him.

The Apostle John wrote:

> In this the love of God was made manifest
> among us, that God sent his only Son into
> the world, so that we might live through
> him.
>
> 1 John 4:9

God's love is manifested among us as Christ's life is intertwined with ours. The value he gives to us ('I love you') and the value we return to him ('I love you too') is received in a union of lives.

We are transformed, by degrees, by this union. Parts of our nature which do not align with his life are cleansed away. Not all at once, but by degree.

Aspects of our humanity that are intertwined with his are nourished and grow. As he progressively manifests himself in us, he heals our humanity from the inside out.

And rather than losing our individual unique personality, we find that God values and dignifies our uniqueness!

Though intertwined, our unique personhood—and his divine Personhood—are kept clearly separate and distinct.

The early church fathers called this "mutual interpenetration with God in Christ, without loss of personhood on either side".

Where do we meet Christ?

In considering the nature of such a wondrous union with God in Christ, a question soon arises: So exactly where in us does he join himself? Where do we meet him?

The astonishing answer is that he joins himself to everything in us.

He meets us not only when we're good—as when we walk into church with a bright smile pasted on our face. He also meets us in the other realities of who we are—as when the whole family is shouting at one another on the way to church!

The Son of God, came to this world in the nature and likeness of our flesh, and joined himself to our humanity. Not just to the good in us, but to the very worst in us as well.

He joins himself to nagging stress, impatience and anxiety. To doubts and unbelief. To our loneliness, insecurity and fear. He knows our rebellion, anger and bitterness.

He joins himself to us when we're stuck at the crossroads. When we try to do the right thing. We're committed to being a better Christian, but our efforts and striving are not sufficient to change our fundamental nature.

We want to walk the good and proper path, but we keep taking that old familiar path. The one that curves us back onto ourselves.

Back to the place where we stand, once again, stuck at the crossroads. And Christ meets us there as well.

The Apostle Paul wrote:

> For what the law was powerless to do because it was weakened by the flesh, God did by sending his own Son in the likeness of sinful flesh to be a sin offering. And so he condemned sin in the flesh.
>
> Romans 8:3

Jesus, the Son of Man, comes to us clothed in our humanity, and meets us in our personal mess.

Consider the young man in the field. He's striving to do what's right. He's working at the holiness the Father requires. But his doing is never good enough.

His anxious labor curves him back onto himself. He's bound up in a transaction between himself and God, which keeps him in the place where he stands in the field alone, exhausted and unchanged.

As he cries out "I can't, I don't know how" Jesus comes into the darkness alongside him. And joins himself completely to him. To everything about him.

Exchanging humanities

But why? Why would Christ assume what's distorted and wrong?

We can understand how he might join himself to the good in us. But to the other stuff we hide from him?!

Because even though Christ fully assumes our brokenness—he is not broken by it! He joins himself to what's wrong in us, but he does not respond to it as we do.

And his not responding as we do makes all the difference for us!

In assuming our weaknesses, Christ penetrates our broken condition. He cleanses our fallen nature from the inside out, and gives us his responses in exchange for ours.

Somehow our condition is not broken! It's good. It's peaceful. We are able to respond rightly. And it didn't come from us! It came from him!

Paul wrote:

> For our sake God made him to be sin who knew no sin, so that in him we might become the righteousness of God.
>> 2 Corinthians 5:21

Saint Hillary of Potiers wrote an insight into this scripture in the 3rd century:

> (Christ) took upon him the flesh in which we have sinned... that by wearing our flesh he might forgive sins; a flesh which he shares with us by wearing it, not by sinning in it.
>> Saint Hillary of Potiers

God knows everything that you and I try to do but cannot do. He is merciful toward our iniquities, and remembers our sins no more. (Hebrews 8:12) He doesn't throw us back on ourselves in order to perform for him. Even in those places where our hearts condemn us, God is greater than our hearts, and he knows all things. (1 John 3:20)

The Apostle John wrote:

> If we confess our sins, he is faithful and just and will forgive us our sins and purify us from all unrighteousness.
>
> 1 John 1:8-9

When you cry out, "Lord I cannot!" Christ says "Yes, you cannot. But I can. Here, try this." And with profound kindness, in your humanity he cleanses you, exchanges his responses for yours, and reconciles you to God.

Christ empowers us in our personal history to new and good responses. Which are truly ours! But they are his! But they are ours!

How does this work out in everyday life? I'd like to share a personal example when Christ met me as I was stuck at a crossroads.

I was in line at the check out counter of our local supermarket, having chosen the shortest queue. There were 4 people ahead of me. An elderly woman was at the front checking out. She slowly fished through her purse, and eventually took out a receipt and gave it to the cashier. The cashier looked at it and they talked for a minute or two. Then the cashier called for a manager.

I looked at the other checkout. About 10 people. I am still ok.

After about a minute the cashier stood up and looked around. Then she bent to the microphone and called out again for a manager.

The four of us in line turned to look at each other. With that shared sense of complaint.

Now I was impatient. I began to think should I go and get the manager? Should I speak out, take charge and fix this offence? Of course for the good of others.

Maybe the store needs me to teach them a lesson.

I had crossed over the line. I was impatient. And I didn't like it.

Instead of my usual reaction—complaining to others, counting to 10, texting on my phone—I took my impatience to Christ.

"Jesus I am impatient, and I don't like it. I don't like this and I don't like it!"

Somehow, immediately I sensed Jesus was in it with me. In my impatience! As if he was saying "Yes this is an impatient situation." He caught me off guard. He understood! Then he said "But look—"

I looked over to the elderly lady at the front of the line, and I *saw* her. She was uncomfortable. She was embarrassed, and a bit slower than the rest. She was poor. She needed some kindness from this world, not judgement.

Buying groceries wasn't as easy for her as it was for the rest of us.

All my impatience left. Instead I felt love and compassion for her. She deserved all the time she needed to get by. And I had all the time in the world to give her.

I "turned" and looked at the Lord in wonder. "Who are you?! My impatience; it's gone! Am I now seeing this elderly lady the way you do?! You're amazing. Who are you that you know me so well?!"

At the checkout counter, on an average day, I was worshiping the Lord Jesus, the light of the world, as he waited his turn in line with me. Being transformed by his marvelous life:

> I have been crucified with Christ. It is no longer I who live, but Christ who lives in me. And the life I now live in the flesh I live by the faith of the Son of God, who loved me and gave himself for me.
>
> Galatians 2:20

All my good and bad deeds

In the 15th century a Scottish theologian wrote:

> I have taken all my good deeds and all
> my bad deeds, and cast them ... in a
> heap before the Lord, and fled from them
> both, and betaken myself to the Lord Jesus
> Christ, and in him I have sweet peace!
>
> David Dickson

Such wise counsel rings like a bell across the centuries. Casting our good deeds, and our bad deeds, in a heap before the Lord. And fleeing from both. Taking ourselves to the Savior who is God's answer to both.

For each time we are touched by a connection with Christ's life, we are changed by the love we receive.

When you're stuck at a crossroads, why not cry out "I can't." Ask him to come to where you're stuck by crying out "I can't. I don't know how."

He understands what you are stuck in. He's with you in your humanity, but he's not at all stuck like you are. May the Savior of the crossroads meet you in your humanity, saying; "No you cannot. But I can." (2 Cor 1:20)

And as Christ gives you his responses in exchange for yours, may the "stuckness" fade away.

May you walk out of the crossroads with him. Delivered. Together. Transformed. Arms intertwined.

Heart and soul restored. Following him in the paths of righteousness which are called by his name. (Psalm 23:3)

Though none of us have yet arrived, it can be that we come to know and understand what home is like.

It's being with him.

The crossroads fade behind us, and the path of life lies before us. We're coming home to our Father.

Jesus is bringing us home.

Chapter Five

THE COMFORT OF SONSHIP

This is a story with a happy ending. It's about a journey into the comfort of sonship.

In a dream sequence, a young boy and a father are driving through the night down an empty desert highway. The car is one of those big vintage American cars, heavy and substantial, with a bench seat.

The man at the wheel is enjoying the journey. The ride is smooth, and the tires are humming. He looks down the highway, glad to have the boy's company.

The boy is not enjoying the ride at all. He feels awkward, nervous, and a bit suspicious. He's not sure why he's in the car, or what he is supposed to do or say to his father.

He leans against the passenger door looking out, keeping one hand on the armrest.

But time passes by, the car is comfortable and smooth, and nothing happens. The boy begins to wonder what's going on. His father seems content, humming every now and then.

Soon the boy asks "Father where are we going?"

"Oh, wait till you see. We're heading to a beautiful spot I know, that's filled with lots of things to see and do. Things to discover and explore, and there are children your age waiting for you."

As he spoke the boy began to imagine what lay before them. A faint hope stirred within and he looked out ahead. Then he turned and looked at his Father. He seemed happy. In control. Glad to be going to the place ahead.

Maybe even glad to have his company?!

The boy moved over next to the Father. He rested his head against his shoulder.

Suddenly a large bump lifted and shook the car. The boy shouted and threw himself out the passenger door.

It is hard to tell how long the boy was gone. Eventually the handle of the passenger door moved. It opened, and the breathless boy pulled himself onto the seat. He shut the door, panting, and clung to its handle.

The Father looked over. He seemed to welcome him back to the seat beside him.

After some time for recovery, the boy's fear subsides. His Father was still the same; constant and present. The boy began to relax, and soon began to enjoy the ride again. He became drowsy, and without realising it had nodded off, his head resting against his Father's side.

His Father put his arm around his shoulder.

Again a massive jolt jarred the car violently from side to side. The boy woke with a shout and flew to the passenger door. He opened it wide.

The darkness swirled below him as he held onto the door. But something inside strengthened him. Wait, pull back. Return to the car. With an effort, he pulled himself back in. He shut the door and clung to it.

The Father quietly looked over at his son.

This time it didn't take as long for the boy to recover.

He soon found himself sidled up against his father. They began sharing stories one after another; with each tale better than the one before.

The Father put his arm around the boy, the boy leaned against him.

Then again the car hit another massive bump. But this time the boy grabbed onto his father's shirt and clung to him. Then he clung harder. And soon the fear subsided; and soon each bump on the journey got smaller and smaller, as the boy rested on the bosom of the Father.

The Father looked upon his son at his side:

> Because he clings to me in love, I will deliver him; I will protect him, because he knows my name. When he calls to me, I will answer him; I will be with him in trouble; I will rescue him and honour him. With long life I will satisfy him and show him my salvation.
>
> Psalm 91:14-16

Driving along, the Father turned to the boy, "You know son, we've already arrived." The boy replied, "What? We're already here? We're still driving. Father, where are we?"

The Father replied, "Look where you are. You're resting next to me, holding fast to me. I am very well pleased to have you at my side."

Then the Father said, "And all the good of you being next to me, is thanks to my Beloved Son."

The boy replied, "Father I don't understand."

The Father explained, "You were anxious at first, but then you began to relax in my presence. When you asked me where we were going, didn't something rise up inside you with hope and possibility? That was my Son, giving you a glimpse of what sons experience with me.

"When you threw yourself out of the car in fear, didn't strength in the darkness help you go back to the car and climb in? That was my Son, revealing to you where you really belong.

"When you were about to throw yourself out again in fear, didn't a strength call you back, to hang on the door and not jump, but to close the door and stay near? That was my Son, showing you that sons stay near.

"When you didn't leave but clung to me in love, it was my Son who showed you that you are with him, next to my bosom.

"My Son strengthened you to stay and not leave, when you wanted to jump away. He made you want to sit by me, and your fears dissolved by my love. So just stay near, and cling to me in love."

The boy didn't understand all that the Father said, but he heard the Son's cry of "Abba! Father" within, calling him to know the comfort of sonship.

He said, "Father, if all I have to do is to cling to you in love, I can do that!" And he snuggled into his Father's side.

And they headed down the road together.

No longer orphans

Of all the blessings that we receive from Christ, perhaps none is more astonishing than to experience the love the Father has for us in his Son.

Jesus knows that without him we are separated from our Father, and he will not allow this desperate state of affairs to continue:

Jesus said "I will not leave you as orphans; I will come to you."

Without the Father we live as orphans, existing without the deep comfort of a father's care, and without a place to call home.

An orphan's life is burdened by a broken relationship between father or mother. Even if their parents are living, a deep alienation and distrust settles upon his soul.

An orphan's thoughts and acts are darkened by convictions of believing no one really understands. No one cares. No one is there for them except themselves.

Having only themselves to survive, an orphan builds a bubble of self-reliance. They survive the world by whatever means possible. Follow the rules, or break the rules. Use whatever they can to their advantage. Take whatever comfort and pleasure they desire.

But if by luck or effort or willpower they do get everything they desire, it still doesn't satisfy. They still lack a deep security.

Orphans can't find home; the place where they can just rest and belong.

Jesus deeply understands and relates to the desolation and loneliness of orphans. When he said "I will not leave you as orphans" he promised to alter their existence.

To give them the home they are searching for.

Joseph

I've come to know a young man from Africa, whom we'll call Joseph. Joseph has travelled through many distant countries, seeking a place he could call home. He had to flee his country; things were violent and quite dark. Joseph has seen and suffered things beyond my ability to perceive. He lives at a homeless shelter, but Joseph is not homeless. He's found home—or rather home found him.

There is a Christian couple serving at the shelter, 'naturally' gifted at loving and connecting with the humanity of street people. Joseph was drawn to them. He sensed something different about this couple; they were consistent, settled, and sincere in their care. They enjoyed Joseph's company, and they began to connect together at the shelter.

One Sunday Joseph accepted their invitation to fellowship with other Christians. As he described it later, he sensed a presence among these people. He said there was something about them that caused him to feel secure and happy.

It made him want to be with them, and to know more about what this presence was.

Soon thereafter my wife and I met Joseph, and he opened his heart to this "new thing" he was experiencing. At one point he said "I know the source of life cannot come from me. I cannot find it in me. It is from the outside. Life must come to me."

That evening Joseph received and believed in the name of Jesus, the Son of the living God. It was wonderful to witness the Messiah calling Joseph home.

Three months later Joseph was baptized in the couple's pool.

His smile radiates the joy of God's presence. There's something about him that makes us lift our eyes to the Source of life.

> I sought the Lord, and he answered me; he delivered me from all my fears. Those who look to him are radiant; their faces are never covered with shame. This poor man called, and the Lord heard him; he saved him out of all his troubles.
>
> Psalm 34:4-8

And now he builds the foundation of his life, day by day, into the knowledge of Christ, as the Spirit teaches him to put on Christ and have no confidence in the flesh.

Sometimes a cloud passes over Joseph's face, as he thinks of his past, and the troubles of his days. But then he's touched by the One who says:

> Fear not I for am with you, be not afraid for I am your God. I will lead you, I will guide you, son. I will strengthen you with my righteous right hand.
>
> Isaiah 41:10

And Joseph's smile quietly returns.

Childlike faith

Jesus leads us into the childlikeness of faith and trust which he has with his heavenly Father.

> And they were bringing children to him that he might touch them, and the disciples rebuked them. But when Jesus saw it, he was indignant and said to them, "Let the children come to me; do not hinder them, for to such belongs the kingdom of God. Truly, I say to you, whoever does not receive the kingdom of God like a child shall not enter it." And he took them in his arms and blessed them, laying his hands on them.
>
> Mark 10:13-16

Look at how the children found God's love. Each came seeking relational contact. They came for a hug and a blessing! Each received that as Christ took them in his arms and laid his hand upon them.

I'm pretty sure they went away feeling loved. That's what trusting children do.

Sons and daughters learn to ask and receive with confidence born of filial trust. It's the trust of a child knowing he or she has been loved and will be loved.

It's an assurance of faith, of leaning into the Father as his son or daughter, and receiving his love in return.

In gathering the children to himself, I believe that Jesus reveals how he depends on his heavenly Father.

The Son of Man abides in childlike faith and trust, seeking the Father for everything. And he receives everything from him.

Asking the Father and receiving from the Father reveals the divine union between God the Father and God the Son.

Christ shares his sonship

Since orphans don't know what it is to have a relationship with a father, they must learn what it's like through experience. They must somehow receive love from a father in order to truly become a son or daughter at heart.

Christ accomplishes this deep transformation! He brings orphans into the very love that the Father has for him!

Jesus prayed to the Father:

> I have made you known to them, and will continue to make you known in order that the love you have for me may be in them and that I myself may be in them.
>
> John 17:26

Christ lifts us into his sonship. He joins us to himself by the Spirit, and gives us the right to become children of God.

Our Father's predetermined plan was to brings orphans into sonship this way. To adopt us through Christ.

The Father therefore sees us not as servants, not as outsiders, but as sons and daughters. We are a family, brought near by our salvation in the Beloved Son.

It takes time for an orphan to believe and trust. It requires waves of revelation to know what it truly means to be a son or daughter. Our hardness of heart, our self-absorption of living for self—it all blocks the truth that a guarded and punitive existence is no longer necessary.

How do we overcome the hardness that keeps us from the Father? Christ accomplishes this for us! By joining us to himself, Christ gives us his love for the Father, which enables us to cry out to the Father with him:

> And because you are sons, God has sent
> the Spirit of his Son into our hearts, crying,
> "Abba! Father!"
>
> Galatians 4:6

Christ's Spirit penetrates our heart with faith, enabling us to believe and trust that the Father loves us as he loves his Beloved Son.

The orphan's fear of punishment is cast out as Christ in us gives us a profound assurance of our Father's love.

His love for the Father softens our hearts and enables us to join him in knowing the Father and receiving his love.

As Jesus loves the Father, so we come to love our Father. With Christ, and through him, we are sons and daughters of God.

Receive the comfort of sonship

Can you hear the Spirit of God's Son in you crying out "Abba! Father"? That's the Spirit of Christ crying out to the Father in you, and with you.

Our longing to know the Father is a response borne out of the Father's longing for you to know him in Christ.

Did you know that you honor the Son when you join him in sonship? Abiding in him in the bosom of our Father?

Did you know that you honor the Father when you come through Christ and cling to him in love as his beloved child?

Joined to Christ, we enter into the comfort of sonship as a child of God.

Enabled to love the Lord with all our heart, soul, mind and strength.

And our Father looks upon you, and puts his arm around your shoulder:

> Because he clings to me in love, I will deliver him; I will protect him, because he knows my name.
>
> When he calls to me, I will answer him; I will be with him in trouble; I will rescue him and honour him.
>
> With long life I will satisfy him and show him my salvation.
>
> Psalm 91:14-16

Chapter Six

RESTFUL INCREASE

I'd like to look once more at the question which my friend sent me, which began this book. Hopefully we'll begin to understand her question in a new light:

> Tom I want to ask a question about receiving God's love. Why, do you think, that it still feels like we are trying to achieve love? Or perhaps it's more an inability to receive it and just ahhhh..., rest in it?
> Is it too much distraction? And then how to get rid of the distraction without making it into a discipline of striving?

Let's look at each of these questions in turn.

I want to ask a question
about receiving God's love

My friend didn't start by asking what she must **do** for God to love her. Doing was not the issue. Right off she was asking about the challenge of receiving. And she was spot on. The primary issue to knowing God's love is learning to receive.

Author James Jordan wrote:

> The key to Christianity is this: If we are to become competent at anything it is this one thing. Learn to become an expert at receiving.

Can you sense the profound relational difference between receiving verses doing? It's worth considering that question deeply, and reflecting on its implications.

Here's a litmus test: how easy is it to let someone care for you?

Is it easier for you to care for others, than it is to let someone care for you?

Do you feel safer keeping people at a distance? Do you find it hard to let down your guard, in order to receive care from others?

I think we all struggle with this in one form or another. The point is, receiving care is harder than it first seems.

Caring for others is easy in comparison.

Why does it still feel like we are trying to achieve love

My friend is asking all the right questions. Yes, it does feel that we're in a process of trying to merit love.

As humans we strive to earn our worth. Our value is wrapped up in what we as humans do. To be affirmed we have to work at it. We have to earn it.

But in our relationship with God, the assumption we have to merit his love is actually the very thing that *hinders* us from receiving it!

What a mysterious paradox. You can't receive God's love if you feel you must perform for it. If I believe I must strive to merit God's love, then I will lose that profound awareness that I am valued by God simply for who I am in his sight. (Isaiah 43:4)

This is such a wonderful, mysterious, divine paradox, that only makes sense through revelation from God's word. Throughout scripture God calls us to cease striving to achieve love, so that we might be open to receive the love we strive for.

Or perhaps it's more an inability to receive

This is another profound insight into our relationship with God. On our own, do we as humans lack some intrinsic *capacity* to actually receive?

It's a deep question worth much reflection. I believe that in our own strength, we are *unable* to receive the love of God.

Scripture tells us that we need God's help in order to receive. He must **enable** us to receive his love—and he has mercifully done just that! By giving us his Son Jesus Christ, God our Father enables us with a new nature to receive love, with a capacity to pour out the love that we receive!

God promised this radical transformation through the prophet Ezekiel:

> And I have given a new heart to you, And I give a new spirit in your midst, And I have turned aside the heart of stone out of your flesh, And I have given a heart of flesh to

you. And I give My Spirit in your midst,
And I have done this, so that you walk in
My statutes, And you keep My judgments,
and have done them.

Ezekiel 36:26-27

We gradually awaken with growing awareness, with faith like the dawning of a new day, that in Christ Jesus the love proclaimed in the gospel is truly ours to receive! We are new creations, with hearts transformed, and God's Spirit abiding within.

And it's a continuous process of being empowered to receive.

In Ephesians 3:14, Paul asks our Father that we "be *strengthened* with power through God's Spirit in your inner being, so that Christ might dwell in your hearts through faith."

Paul asks for that continuous *strengthening* by God's Spirit, to know and to receive the flow of love that comes to us through the Spirit within us.

And to just ahhhh... rest in it

And what we do as the Spirit strengthens us with power to receive?!

We step into the love by faith and just, ahhhh... rest in it.

Consider the many scriptures that promise this great blessing:

> There remains, then, a Sabbath rest for the people of God. For whoever enters God's rest also rests from his own work, just as God did from his.
>
> Hebrews 4:9

Entering God's rest. Knowing the living peace. The ever flowing goodness.

The work has been done. We rest from our work, just as God did from his.

Peace I leave with you; my peace I give to you. Not as the world gives do I give to you. Let not your hearts be troubled, neither let them be afraid.

John 14:27

Peace like a river. The peace of Christ. The peace that is his divine nature being given to us, to become our peace.

As the Father has loved me, so have I loved you. Abide in my love.

John 15:9

The love that Christ experiences from the Father, is the same love that he has for you.

He assures us of it. Then he calls us to abide in his love.

It's so simple. We make it complicated when we strive.

But by his power we are given an ability to receive. And as we learn to receive, it becomes easier to receive more.

Is it too much distraction

Yes it's absolutely way too much distraction!

The fears, worries, shrill voices of the world. They are incredibly distracting.

Responsibilities, suffering, stress. Fear of failing, fear of missing out. The imposter syndrome. Hurting others. Guilt, shame.

> Martha, Martha ...you are worried and upset about many things. But only one thing is necessary. Mary has chosen the good portion, and it will not be taken away from her.
>
> Luke 10:41-42

Distractions cause us to react out of self sufficiency. It's a human reflex. We turn in on ourselves, to deal with the stress. We complain about others.

Like Martha we are worried and upset about many things. It's all incredibly distracting.

◆》 ⋅⋅◆⋅⋅ 《◆

And how to eliminate distraction
without it becoming a discipline of striving

> Now to one who works, wages are not
> reckoned as a gift but as something due.
> But to one who does not work but trusts
> him who justifies the ungodly, such faith
> is reckoned as righteousness.
>
> Romans 4:4-5

We don't strive to eliminate distractions. We take our distractions to the One who is able to eliminate them for us! The distractions are worked out of us by the Savior.

We trust him to do this in us. In fact the faith that causes us to ask and receive from God all that we cannot do, is considered by God to be righteousness.

Dear reader, through Christ you are able to receive God's love. Without doing anything for it.

You can ask for power to receive. You're asking for the immense privilege of living in union with Christ.

So ask the Holy Spirit to continuously strengthen you with power, to enable you to know the love which surpasses knowledge.

It's praying with Paul along these lines:

> *Father God strengthen me with power, through your Spirit in my inner being.*
>
> *Holy Spirit strengthen me with power to receive and believe, so that Christ my Lord might dwell in my heart through faith—so that I would be rooted and grounded in love, and would have strength to know the astounding love of Christ which surpasses knowledge.*
>
> *Thank you. Amen.*

In the kingdom of God, our Father desires that you receive his love. To know that you're valued, and it's his good pleasure to give you the kingdom.

Awaken to this transformation. To unfolding revelations, as God strengthens you with his power by the Holy Spirit to receive and to believe his love.

Indeed, resting to receive is such a mystery, because it's an intimate knowledge which surpasses knowledge.

But that doesn't mean it's not true.

Christ is completing a good work in you. He is giving you faith to know that your sonship is secure in him.

So just learn to .... ahhhh ...receive.

Enter that restful increase, where all your being, and all your doing, is reconciled by belonging.

Chapter Seven

GOD WANTS YOU FOR YOU

We learn to draw life daily from Christ by asking ourselves a highly practical decision: do I choose to pursue life on my own today? Drawing from my own resources?

Or do I go to Christ and receive life from him, in order to live from him. To be with him in whatever the day brings?

When I look to do life out of self sufficiency, I'm seeking to live from what I can gain or lose in this world.

But when I look to Christ and ask for life, what I receive is *relationship*. And it is a relationship with the living God which satisfies.

Because of the deep relational blessing of living through Christ, we soon lose the need of wanting so much out of this world.

So go do what Christ says—go to him and drink! And not just a little sip. Drink until the thirst is gone.

Drink until the emptiness of life without him is filled by the abundance of life with him.

The more you receive of him, the more you want *him!* More even than his blessings.

Sure we love his blessings and we're so grateful he gives so much.

But we want to know Jesus, the Giver of gifts, more than we want his gifts.

Spending time and speaking

The risen Lord Jesus relates to us in our ordinary, everyday humanity. He joins himself to who we are, not who we ought to be. He offers relationship with the "real you".

Because God wants to connect, you can go to Scripture and view it as a relational lens, through which God speaks to you.

This may seem obvious, but how often do we open the Bible more as an instructional text-book, instead of a personal letter, addressed to us? A letter which speaks in a personal way, compelling us to actively listen because it's his words we're hearing.

Verse after verse opens up to relationship. His word invites us in, teaching us truths in a way that no human institution can replicate.

In a very real way, scripture speaks to us in the person of God.

Since God is interested in spending time and speaking with you, and not the polished presentation of yourself, go to the place where you're most naturally yourself and listen to him.

Go to where it's easiest to receive, to where there is less distraction. Where opening the space of yourself to him feels most natural.

My wife loves to walk in the mountains. She looks for just the right vista, then she stops and then listens to the silence. Looking across the hills and valleys, the Presence of the Good Shepherd meets her, speaks with her, and restores her soul.

I spend time with God with instrumental music in the background. A friend who is an opera singer cannot have music on when she's with the Lord; it distracts her because she focuses on the music.

There is no set formula as to what's natural. Only you know where you naturally hear him. Music, walking, surfing, knitting. Gardening.

Ask for his love

With childlikeness, ask him to love you. Not for anything you do, but for who you are.

Step into being a secure child, who is coming to dad for a hug.

Go be loved, where you most need his love. Gently and kindly loved.

He knows you need his love. His loves gives you intrinsic value and worth. It casts out fear.

It builds you up, with strength and encouragement.

It gives you quiet confidence. It sows light and truth in you.

It casts out darkness.

Where you are weak the Lord says:

> My grace is sufficient for you, for my power is made perfect in weakness.
> 2 Corinthians 12:9

Our heavenly Father declares "When I am with you in your weakness, you are with me in my strength."

So go and ask Abba Father for a hug:

>*Lord I come to you and ask for your love. Thank you that I don't have to earn your love.*

>*please pour your love into me. Do that which is pleasing to you to renew my heart and mind.*

>*As you work, fill me with a deep assurance and living hope—that you have taken me to yourself, to abide in your house forever.*

>*Amen.*

Resist the bully

There's a spirit of this world, which is at work in the sons of disobedience. (Ephesians 2:2)

It demands that we live on our own, separated and apart from Christ.

The world's cares and distractions—responsibilities, desires, control, power, lust, glory—are all designed to choke the Word and separate us from Christ.

We're getting sick of being bullied into being separated.

We all together say "No!" to the bully.

Instead of our knee-jerk reaction to live out of self, we use that pressure to run to the Lord!

Take the pressure to Christ and tell him what's besetting your humanity.

Tell him and don't take it on your own. Unload. Let him assume your pressure.

In other words, don't take the stress of life to yourself

alone! Take the pressure to the Lord and tell him about how it's making you react.

Soon those distractions will fade away, as you receive his life and truth that casts out the lies of the enemy.

Don't let the enemy's accusations and lies cause you to separate in fear from God.

Our Father never calls his children to leave his side, in order to get closer to him. It makes no sense!

He says come, stay near:

> I will instruct you and teach you in the way you should go; I will counsel you with my eye upon you.
>
> Be not like a horse or a mule, without understanding, which must be curbed with bit and bridle, or it will not stay near you.
> Psalm 32:8-9

Hear the wise, pure, and peaceable voice (James 3:16)—the voice of our Good Shepherd.

Calling you by name.

Finding your life with him in the sacred space of his love.

> My sheep listen to my voice; I know them, and they follow me.
>
> I give them eternal life, and they will never perish.
>
> No one can snatch them out of my hand.
>
> My Father who has given them to me is greater than all. No one can snatch them out of my Father's hand.
>
> John 10:27-29

A closing prayer

There's something within our humanity, that fears we might lose the kingdom. That we must earn it, or do something to maintain it's presence. Lest it leave, and leave us to fend for ourselves.

This fear is a phantom from an orphan past.

We know it. But the background doubt keeps us from resting in the solid foundation that it is our Father's good pleasure to give us the kingdom.

So much of our life has been apart...we fear being apart again.

So much of our life has been spent hiding...we fear that God has left, even though it is we who have curved back in on ourselves.

There is a space in the heart of man, where Christ comes to dwell by the Spirit of truth. The inner being is awakened to join in a relationship which is constant, which never sleeps, which never ceases, and which never ends.

Where man's inner being was once singular, bound and of itself, man's inner being now awakens into an invitation of relationship with a Person so much greater than itself.

Thoughts and emotions, understanding and responses are redefined by hearing and sharing with him. He relates so closely to our flesh and blood that you could say he abides with us and is in us.

So closely, that life with him becomes essential for life itself.

By degrees, he causes us to come alive as recreated humans in his divine humanity. Humanity which he gives to us in eternal communion with him.

We soon learn to no longer regard ourselves as persons alone, stuck on an island of self, apart from God. By the gift of faith we begin to understand that we are constantly joined somehow to Christ, in a relationship that defines how we are to see ourselves.

For in that relationship—of knowing God and being known by him—we are understood, we are believed in, and we are loved.

In the mystery of God's transcendent goodness we experience by faith that we matter very much to him.

We are loved into newness of life by his love.

We leave behind the fear and striving of loneliness, and awaken to living hope in the knowledge that Christ has come to us.

That we might live with him—by living through him.

Dear Savior and Lord, thank you for nourishing us and cherishing us as your very own.

Oh may our lives be filled with the fullness of yours, Lord Jesus.

May our responses come from responses that flow from the wellsprings of your eternal life.

And may the goodness of this all resolve into seeing your face Lord Jesus.

We seek your face O Lord.

Thank you for loving us into life.

Amen.

Epilogue

D ear reader,

This book has only touched the surface of relationship and communion with God. There is so much more of God's love to know and experience in its many unfolding dimensions (Eph 3:14-19) .

As you journey may I encourage you to go back and camp out in those areas of the book where God is speaking to you. What is God revealing to you personally? Is the word of God bringing you life as the Spirit progressively reveals Christ in you?

May I encourage you to share these thoughts and testimony with friends. It is such a blessing to share the life of Christ with one another, in a safe place that is filled with hope and life and transformation.

At Loved into Life, we are planning a series of devotionals called *Continuing Thoughts*, which will continue the vibrant conversation about knowing and experiencing God's love. You can find out more by subscribing to our newsletter at lovedintolife.com.

As you journey on may the Lord continue to bless you, with his nearness being your greatest good.

May you come to know and receive in ever greater measure the eternal life that God has prepared for you in Christ Jesus our Lord.

Love and blessings,

Tom White

ABOUT THE AUTHOR

Tom White

Tom White is my father, and I am privileged to write about him.

Dad possesses a remarkable gift for nurturing and supporting those who, in turn, care for others. Over the years, he has provided leadership and support for many leaders globally, spanning churches, home churches, and those without a church.

He has a pastoral ability to perceive others as God the Father does, guiding individuals to recognize their inherent worth and unique gifts in God's eyes.

Dad has given his life to understanding, encouraging, and inspiring believers to embrace the hope, rest, and purpose that God eagerly desires for them.

Mom and Dad now live in France, where they're serving as pastors helping build churches in the south of France.

My father has dedicated this book to everyone who longs to be loved into life. My prayer is that you not only come to know him through his words but, more importantly, that you deepen your connection with your heavenly Father.

Jeremy White

Printed in Great Britain
by Amazon